MASTERING PROFESSIONAL NETWORKING

MASTERING PROFESSIONAL NETWORKING

42 BEST STRATEGIES

JASMINE WILLIAMS

TABLE OF CONTENTS

INTRODUCTION

Welcome to "Mastering Professional Networking: 42 Best Strategies," the comprehensive guide designed to transform you into a networking maestro. Whether you're a fresh-faced graduate diving into the job market, a seasoned professional aiming to expand your influence, or an entrepreneur forging new pathways, this book is your navigator through the bustling world of career connections.

Networking—it's a buzzword that echoes through the corridors of professional growth, yet its depth is often misunderstood. It's more than exchanging business cards or collecting LinkedIn connections; it's an art, the delicate dance of relationship-building that, when performed with finesse, can open doors to a multitude of opportunities.

Let's embark on this journey together. Through each chapter, we'll explore vital facets of networking with an emphasis on practicality, engagement, and fact-based insights—they are your ammunition for the networking arena. Imagine this book as your treasure map, with every chapter pinpointing a crucial stop on your route to networking treasure. Let's walk through some of the pivotal stops we'll be visiting:

- **Cultivating a Networking Mindset:** Begin your journey by planting your networking roots deep into fertile soil, embracing the mindset essential for authentic and effective connections.

- **Defining Your Networking Goals:** It's time to set your compass. Understand why you're networking and what you aim to achieve, moving beyond superficial exchanges.

- *Crafting an Unforgettable Personal Brand:* Learn to paint a self-portrait that leaves a lasting impression, allowing your essence to shine in every encounter.

- *Elevator Pitches:* Perfect the art of brevity and impact, crafting an introduction that's both memorable and genuine.

- *Listening in Networking:* Discover the power behind the pause, the listening space where true connections are fostered.

Enumerated and bullet-pointed, these are just glimpses of the wealth of knowledge ahead. Each chapter will serve as a strategy session where we dissect, analyze, and build upon core networking principles. We'll uncover the nuances of online networking, the subtleties of non-verbal communication, and the wisdom in handling rejection.

In the spirit of practicality, let's consider an analogy. Networking can be likened to a garden. It requires the right tools—a trowel for sharing your personal brand, the fertilizer of effective communication, and the water of ongoing engagement. Prepare to tend to this garden with intention and regular care, and watch as it flourishes into a lush landscape of professional relationships.

As we proceed, we'll share anecdotes—like the time a simple "hello" led to a pivotal career breakthrough or how a well-timed follow-up forged a lifetime mentorship. You'll find these stories laced with both inspiration and hard-earned wisdom.

Rest assured, this book is your ally. Keep its pages within arm's reach, whether in your office, during your commute, or as part of your nightstand musings. Networking is not confined to conference rooms or formal events; it's an omnipresent aspect of your professional walkabout.

Get ready to transform the way you view and practice networking. Let's journey beyond perfunctory pleasantries and towards meaningful professional kinships. This isn't just about making connections—it's about making the right connections and nurturing them to their fullest potential.

Let "Mastering Professional Networking: 42 Best Strategies" be the catalyst for your networking evolution. It's time to turn the page and step into a world where your network is your net worth. Shall we?

CULTIVATING A NETWORKING MINDSET: EMBRACING CONNECTION

The Key Ideas

Networking is about more than exchanging business cards or adding contacts on LinkedIn. It's about cultivating a genuine interest in others, forging connections that are both meaningful and mutually beneficial. A networking mindset is a proactive attitude, focused on building relationships. It's about seeing every person, not as a means to an end, but as an individual with unique insights and experiences.

Recognize the Value: Understand every interaction is an opportunity to learn and grow. Each person you meet can offer a unique perspective or skill that could be pivotal in your professional journey.

Seek to Contribute: Approach networking with the intention to help others. Offering assistance or resources without immediate expectation of return builds trust and establishes a foundation for reciprocal support.

Practice Listening: Great networkers are not just great talkers; they are great listeners. They know the importance of hearing and understanding others' needs and goals, which allows for more meaningful connections.

Practical Implementation

To apply these ideas, start by:

1. **Reframing Your Approach**:

    ○ View networking events as learning opportunities instead of performance tasks.

    ○ Be curious about what others are involved in. This curiosity can lead to new knowledge and unexpected collaborations.

2. **Setting Goals**:

    ○ Prioritize quality of connections over quantity. Establish a goal to have a certain number of meaningful conversations rather than collecting business cards.

3. **Offering Value**:

    ○ Prepare a mental inventory of your skills, experience, and networks before attending networking events.

    ○ Be ready to share your resources with others.

4. **Fostering Authenticity**:

    ○ Be genuine in your interactions. Authenticity fosters trust and long-term connections.

5. **Consistent Follow-Up**:

    ○ Send a personalized message after meeting someone new. Mention a memorable part of your conversation to reinforce the connection.

6. **Leveraging Social Media**:

   ◦ Use platforms like LinkedIn to engage with your network. Share content that is relevant to your connections and start conversations online.

7. **Engagement in Diverse Settings**:

   ◦ Diversify your networking environments to include conferences, volunteer activities, and online forums, exposing you to a broader range of individuals.

Consistency and Evaluation

A networking mindset requires regular practice and reflection:

- **Integrate Networking Into Your Routine**: Block out time in your schedule for networking activities. Be consistent with your efforts, whether it's attending events or reaching out to connections.

- **Evaluate Your Relationships**: Periodically assess the health of your professional relationships. Ask yourself who you've helped recently and how you've contributed to your network.

- **Seek Feedback**: Request feedback from trusted connections on how you come across. Are you perceived as helpful, knowledgeable, and approachable?

- **Adapt and Evolve**: Stay open to adjusting your approach. Networking is dynamic; what works today may not be as effective tomorrow.

In conclusion, embracing connection means developing a networking mindset that prioritizes authenticity, continuous learning, and mutual benefit. It's an ongoing commitment to cultivating relationships that not only advance your career but also enrich your professional life.

DEFINING YOUR NETWORKING GOALS: BEYOND THE BUSINESS CARD

The Key Ideas

Define Clear Networking Objectives

Your networking efforts must stem from articulate objectives. Ask yourself what you aim to achieve:

- Gain industry insights

- Foster collaborations

- Career progression

- Mentorship opportunities

Understanding Your Value Proposition

Know what you offer to the table. Self-awareness fuels meaningful exchanges:

- Your expertise and skills

- Problem-solving abilities

- Unique perspectives or ideas

- A robust and diverse network

Targeted Networking

Forge relationships that align with your goals:

- Industry leaders and influencers

- Potential mentors or partners

- Peers with complementary skills

Quality Over Quantity

Deep, authentic connections trump a stack of superficial contacts:

- Prioritize depth in conversations

- Follow-up with personalized messages

- Offer help before asking for a favor

Practical Implementation

Research and Preparation

- Identify key individuals and organizations

- Understand their challenges and achievements

- Craft a tailored approach for each

Crafting Your Message

- Elevate your pitch to resonate with your audience's needs

- Convey your unique value succinctly

Engage in the Right Venues

- Select networking events strategically

- Utilize online platforms efficiently

- Engage in relevant industry forums and discussions

Networking Tools

- Organize contacts with a CRM or a personal system

- Leverage social media to maintain presence and engage

Consistency and Evaluation

Regular Networking Activities

- Schedule consistent networking slots in your calendar

- Engage in continuous learning and industry updates

Track Your Progress

- Set milestones for your networking objectives

- Regularly review your contacts and the quality of interactions

Adjustment and Flexibility

- Be prepared to pivot your approach based on outcomes

- Remain open to unexpected opportunities

Seek Feedback

- Ask for constructive criticism from trusted networking contacts

- Continuously hone your interpersonal and communication skills

Networking is not a numbers game of collecting contacts; it's about cultivating a garden of well-tended relationships that grow over time. Define your goals, understand your value, and engage meaningfully. With these principles, the business card is just the beginning.

CRAFTING AN UNFORGETTABLE PERSONAL BRAND

The Key Ideas

- **Personal Brand Foundation**: Your personal brand is a unique combination of skills, experiences, and personality that you want the world to see. It is the telling of your story, and the impression that people gain from your online presence, conversations, and behavior.

- **Clarity of Purpose**: Define what you are passionate about, what you stand for, and your unique value proposition. Know your target audience and shape your brand around what you want to be known for in your professional life.

- **Visual Identity**: Create a consistent visual style across all platforms. This includes a professional headshot, a recognizable logo or monogram, and a cohesive color scheme.

- **Online Presence**: Build a professional profile on LinkedIn, a personal website, and maintain an active presence on other relevant social media platforms.

- **Content Creation**: Establish yourself as a thought leader by regularly producing content relevant to your expertise and industry.

• **Networking**: Engage with industry leaders and potential clients. Attend events, join professional groups, and contribute to discussions.

• **Personal Style and Communication**: How you dress and communicate adds to your personal brand. Ensure that your personal style reflects your professional goals and brand identity.

Practical Implementation

1. **Self-Assessment**: List your strengths, weaknesses, and any unique attributes that set you apart from others. This insight forms the basis of your personal branding strategy.

2. **Define Your Audience**: Determine who you want to reach with your brand. Tailor your language, tone, and content to resonate with this group.

3. **Craft Your Message**: What key ideas do you want to communicate about who you are and what you stand for? Make them clear, focused, and concise.

4. **Design Your Brand Elements**:

   ○ Choose a professional font and color palette.

   ○ Design or commission a personal logo.

   ○ Have a quality, professional headshot taken.

5. **Launch Your Online Presence**:

   ○ Build or update your LinkedIn profile with a compelling summary and experience section.

   ○ Create or revamp your personal website to showcase your portfolio, blog, or bio.

○ Use the same profile picture and branding across all platforms for consistency.

6. **Develop a Content Strategy**:

   ○ Decide on content types: blog posts, podcasts, videos, etc.

   ○ Create a content calendar to plan your publishing schedule.

   ○ Share your content on social media and in professional circles.

7. **Engagement Plan**:

   ○ Identify networking events and conferences to attend.

   ○ Determine online groups and forums to join.

   ○ Plan how often you will interact with others in your field.

Consistency and Evaluation

- **Maintain a Consistent Brand**: Ensure that your messaging and visual identity are uniform across all channels and that you adhere to your content schedule.

- **Measure Your Impact**:

   ○ Track metrics on your website and social media platforms.

   ○ Seek feedback from peers and mentors.

- **Iterate and Evolve**: Your brand should grow with your career. Regularly assess and adjust your approach as you gain new experiences, skills, and goals.

- **Annual Review**: Set aside time each year to review your personal branding goals and strategy, making adjustments as necessary.

Remember, building a personal brand doesn't happen overnight. It requires dedication, consistency, and the willingness to promote oneself authentically. Your personal brand is a living asset; nurture it, and it will open doors to new opportunities and professional growth.

ELEVATOR PITCHES: HOW TO INTRODUCE YOURSELF EFFECTIVELY

The Key Ideas

An elevator pitch is a brief, persuasive speech that you can use to spark interest in what you, or your organization, do. It should be concise, lasting no more than 30 seconds to 2 minutes – about the duration of an elevator ride.

- **Clarity is paramount.** Your introduction must be understandable by anyone in your professional field or beyond. This leaves no room for jargon or complex terms.

- **Brevity is non-negotiable.** Your pitch should get straight to the point, focusing on who you are, what you do, and what your goal or unique value proposition is.

- **Passion is infectious.** When you speak about your work or your goals, let your excitement show. It draws people in and makes them curious.

- **Customize for your audience.** Tailor your speech to align with the interests and needs of the person or group you are addressing.

• **Action-oriented conclusion.** End with a clear call-to-action such as requesting a meeting, exchanging business cards, or offering a follow-up conversation.

Practical Implementation

Creating an effective elevator pitch follows a structured path. Here's how to craft yours:

1. **Start with a strong introduction.** Use your name and what you do in a way that imparts value, not just your job title.

2. **Identify the problem you solve.** Make it relatable to your listener, showing why it's significant.

3. **Present your unique value proposition.** Explains how you address this problem differently and successfully.

4. **Mention your goals.** Align them with the interests of your listener.

5. **Close with a clear call-to-action.** What do you want as a result of this pitch?

Example Structure of an Elevator Pitch:

1. Hook: "Hi, I'm Jane Doe, I turn complex data into easy-to-understand stories."

2. Problem: "Businesses often drown in data without gaining insights."

3. Solution: "I specialize in data visualization that informs strategic decisions."

4. Outcome: "I've helped several Fortune 500 companies increase their ROI through effective data presentations."

5. Call-to-action: "Let's schedule a call to explore how I can help your team."

Consistency and Evaluation

Practicing your pitch is crucial. Regular rehearsal ensures you're ready to present it naturally and confidently at any time. This also allows you to refine your pitch to best fit different audiences and situations.

- **Seek feedback regularly.** Encourage others to critique your pitch for content, clarity, and delivery.

- **Adjust and evolve.** As your skills, experiences, and goals change, so should your pitch.

- **Record your success rate.** Keep track of when your pitch results in a follow-up action, and use this data to improve.

- **Stay authentic.** Your pitch should reflect your true professional identity and aspirations.

Remember, each interaction is a chance to evolve your pitch and improve your introduction. Crafting an effective elevator pitch is an iterative process; it's never 'finished', but always developing as you grow as a professional.

THE POWER OF LISTENING IN NETWORKING

The Key Ideas

Active Listening is the Foundation: In the realm of networking, active listening forms the bedrock of meaningful connections. It's about genuinely hearing what the other person is saying, discerning the nuances of their speech, and responding thoughtfully.

- **Body Language Speaks Volumes**: Simple non-verbal cues such as nodding or maintaining eye contact can signify engagement.

- **Questions Are Your Best Tools**: Open-ended questions encourage a dialogue, revealing deeper insights into a person's experiences and needs.

- **Listen to Understand, Not to Reply**: Focus on their words, not on what you'll say next. This fosters trust and rapport.

Silence Can Be Golden: Give the speaker room to express themselves. It signals respect for their ideas and can lead to more comprehensive communication.

Empathy Amplifies Connections: Empathetic reactions resonate at a personal level. When you empathize, it demonstrates that you are not just hearing, but feeling the conversation.

Reciprocity in Dialogue: Remember, mutual exchanges pave the way for stronger connections. Sharing your own stories in response to theirs can create a balanced and engaging dialogue.

Practical Implementation

1. **Begin with the Right Mindset**: Approach each conversation with a genuine curiosity about the other person. Assume each person you meet has something valuable to teach you.

2. **Employ the 'PARA' Technique**: Pause, Ask, Reflect, Answer. This method ensures you are giving appropriate space and consideration to the conversation.

3. **Mindful Listening Exercises**: Daily, take time to practice listening to a friend, family member, or colleague without interruption. Reflect on what was said and how it felt to fully engage.

4. **Feedback Loops**: Occasionally, paraphrasing or summarizing what the other person said helps validate their thoughts and ensures clarity in communication.

5. **Networking Events Focus**: At events, challenge yourself to remember specific details about those you speak with—reference these details in your follow-up communications.

Consistency and Evaluation

Track Your Progress: Keep a journal to note improvements and areas needing work. Reflect on the quality of your interactions and identify patterns where your listening skills effectively fostered new connections.

Request Honest Feedback: Sometimes, perception is not reality. Ask close professional contacts how they view your conversational skills and be open to constructive criticism.

Set Specific Goals: Aim for tangible objectives, such as meeting with at least two people a week to practice your listening skills, or attending one networking event a month with the goal of having meaningful conversations.

By embracing the power of listening, your networking will transform from a series of transactional encounters into a web of profound professional relationships. This is not about quick fixes or the superficial exchange of business cards—it's about building lasting connections that benefit all parties involved, crafted through the simple, but profound act of truly listening.

ONLINE NETWORKING: LEVERAGING SOCIAL MEDIA PLATFORMS

The Key Ideas

Understanding Your Platforms: Each social media platform has its own culture and methods of interaction. LinkedIn, Twitter, Facebook, and Instagram cater to different audiences and therefore require tailored approaches for effective networking.

Building a Professional Profile: Your profile is your digital handshake. Make it count. Ensure it is up-to-date, professional, and reflective of your personal brand.

Strategic Connections: Connect with purpose. Seek out individuals and groups in your industry or field of interest. Quality trumps quantity.

Engaging Content: Share and create content that is valuable to your network. This positions you as a thought leader and initiates conversations.

Direct Outreach: Sometimes direct messages can open doors. Be respectful, concise, and personalize every message.

Practical Implementation

- **Optimize Profiles:** Ensure your profile picture, bio, and background reflect your professional image. Use keywords relevant to your industry for better search visibility.

- **Follow Industry Leaders:** Gain insights and stay updated on trends by following thought leaders and influencers in your field.

- **Join Groups and Forums:** Platforms such as LinkedIn and Facebook have groups for almost every profession where you can share insights and ask questions.

- **Regular Updates:** Share updates on your professional milestones to keep your network informed and engaged.

- **Interact with Content:** Like, comment, and share relevant posts. This activity shows you're active and engaged with your industry.

- **Virtual Networking Events:** Attend webinars and online conferences to meet new contacts and learn about your industry.

Consistency and Evaluation

- **Establish a Routine:** Dedicate a set amount of time each week to engaging with your social media networks.

- **Set Goals:** Determine what you want to achieve with online networking, such as learning new skills, finding job opportunities, or growing your network.

- **Measure Progress:** Track the growth of your connections, engagements, and the quality of interactions. Adjust your strategy accordingly.

• **Feedback Loop:** Ask for feedback from connections and peers to refine your approach and ensure your interactions are positive and valuable.

Remember, effective online networking is not just about connecting; it's about building relationships that matter and can help propel your career forward.

NETWORKING ETIQUETTE: THE UNSPOKEN RULES

The Key Ideas

Networking, at its core, is the practice of building and maintaining relationships. It's a blend of social finesse, professionalism, and strategic communication. Here's how to navigate its subtleties effectively:

- **First Impressions:** Your introduction sets the tone. A confident handshake and eye contact can go a long way.

- **Active Listening:** Show genuine interest by actively listening and engaging in the conversation.

- **Reciprocity:** Networking is a two-way street—be ready to help others as they help you.

- **Follow-Up:** The true strength of a connection often lies in timely and thoughtful follow-ups after initial meetings.

- **Respect Boundaries:** Recognize and respect personal and professional boundaries within your network.

Practical Implementation

1. **Prepare an Elevator Pitch:** Have a clear and concise statement about your professional role and objectives ready for new introductions.

   - Keep it under 30 seconds

   - Focus on what you can offer, not just what you need

2. **Practice Active Listening:**

   - Nod, maintain eye contact, and ask questions

   - Repeat or paraphrase to show understanding

3. **Effective Communication:**

   - Use clear, jargon-free language

   - Be conscious of body language

4. **Networking Events:**

   - Arrive early to settle in

   - Set a goal for connections you intend to make

5. **Business Card Etiquette:**

   - Offer your card at the end of a conversation

   - Treat received cards with respect

6. **Social Media Interaction:**

   - Keep professional profiles updated

   - Engage with your connections' content thoughtfully

7. **Follow-Up Strategies:**

   - Send personalized messages referring to your conversation

- Propose a concrete next step or meeting

Consistency and Evaluation

Build these practices into your regular networking routine:

- **Maintain a Schedule:** Allocate specific times each week for networking activities.

- **Track Interactions:** Keep a log of contacts, interactions, and follow-ups.

- **Seek Feedback:** After meetings, reflect on what went well and areas for improvement.

- **Adjust as Needed:** Tailor your approach based on the nature of each relationship and feedback received.

Regular evaluation of your networking strategy and etiquette is crucial for continuous improvement. Set periodic reviews to assess the quality of your connections and the outcomes of your networking efforts.

THE ROLE OF MENTORSHIP IN PROFESSIONAL GROWTH

The Key Ideas

Mentorship plays a pivotal role in navigating the complexities of professional arenas. It's a partnership where knowledge and experiences are shared, providing a scaffold for personal and career development.

- **Personalized Guidance**: A mentor offers insights tailored to your specific career path, facilitating growth in a way that generalized advice cannot.

- **Networking Opportunities**: Access to your mentor's professional network can open doors that might otherwise remain closed.

- **Skill Enhancement**: Regular interactions with a mentor can rapidly improve your skill set, from technical abilities to soft skills like leadership and communication.

- **Psychological Support**: A mentor can act as a sounding board for your ideas and worries, providing emotional backing and bolstering your confidence.

Practical Implementation

To leverage mentorship, you need a structured approach, ensuring both mentor and mentee reap the maximum benefit.

1. **Identifying the Right Mentor:**

   ○ Look for compatibility in personality and style.

   ○ Seek out a mentor whose career trajectory you admire.

   ○ Ensure they have the time and willingness to commit.

2. **Setting Objectives:**

   ○ Be clear about your goals.

   ○ Discuss these with your mentor to establish a common understanding.

   ○ Create a road map with milestones.

3. **Engaging in the Relationship:**

   ○ Schedule regular meetings.

   ○ Be prepared with issues, questions, and updates on progress.

   ○ Be open to feedback and willing to act on it.

4. **Giving Back:**

   ○ Offer assistance to your mentor where possible.

   ○ The relationship should be reciprocal, not transactional.

Consistency and Evaluation

Mentorship is a dynamic, ongoing process. It's important to review the arrangement regularly to ensure both parties remain aligned with the set goals.

- **Consistency:**

  - Hold consistent meetings, whether weekly, bi-weekly, or monthly.

  - Commit to actionable steps between meetings.

- **Evaluation:**

  - Periodically assess if the relationship is fulfilling the goals.

  - Be responsive to the need for adjustment in the mentoring plan.

In conclusion, mentorship can be a powerful accelerant to professional growth. Embrace it with intention and commitment, and you'll unlock potential you might never have discovered on your own.

INFORMATIONAL INTERVIEWS: UNLOCKING INDUSTRY INSIGHTS

The Key Ideas

An informational interview is a strategic meeting where you seek advice rather than employment. It's a chance to learn more about a particular job sector, company, or role directly from someone inside.

Understand the Purpose of Informational Interviews

• **Gain Industry Insights**: Get firsthand knowledge about your field of interest from experienced professionals.

• **Build Your Network**: Establish connections that could potentially lead to job opportunities.

• **Clarify Your Career Path**: Learn what skills and experiences are necessary to thrive in your desired career.

• **Foster Mentor Relationships**: Cultivate contacts who might become mentors offering guidance and support.

Selecting the Right People to Interview

- Find professionals who are currently in roles or at companies you aspire to.

- Use LinkedIn and other professional networks to identify potential interviewees.

- Reach out to alumni from your school or professional groups who share your career interests.

Preparing for the Interview

- Research the industry, company, and interviewee thoroughly.

- Prepare a list of tailored, open-ended questions to maximize the information you receive.

- Plan your attire and arrival time; professionalism is key even in a casual setting.

Practical Implementation

Reaching Out for an Interview

1. **Craft Your Message**: Send a personalized request that explains your interest without demanding too much time.

Example:

Subject: Request for Informational Interview from an Aspiring Marketing Professional

Dear [Name],

My name is [Your Name], and I am currently exploring different career paths in the marketing industry. I came across your profile, and I am impressed by your experience in [specific area]. I would greatly appreciate the opportunity to learn more about your journey and gain insights into the field. Would you be available for a 20-30 minute informational interview at your convenience?

I am flexible with scheduling and can adjust to your time frame. Thank you for considering my request, and I look forward to the possibility of speaking with you.

Best Regards, [Your Name]

1. **Arrange the Meeting**: Opt for coffee or a virtual chat—whichever is more convenient for the professional you are interviewing.

During the Interview

- Start with small talk to build rapport.

- Ask your prepared questions; be curious and genuinely interested.

- Listen attentively, taking notes if appropriate.

- Respect their time; keep track of the duration of your meeting.

After the Interview

- Send a thank you note within 24 hours to express your appreciation.

- Reflect on what you learned: write down any new insights and how they might impact your career choices.

- Keep in touch periodically without being overbearing; share updates on your career progress.

Consistency and Evaluation

Establish a Routine

- Aim to conduct at least one informational interview each month.

- Regularly review and refresh your list of potential interviewees.

- Stay updated on industry trends to ask relevant and insightful questions.

Evaluating Your Progress

- Set measurable goals: number of interviews, new insights gained, and connections made.

- After every few interviews, reassess your career goals and the effectiveness of the meetings in advancing your understanding and network.

- Seek feedback from interviewees on how you could improve your approach.

- Track your professional growth and opportunities that arise from these interviews.

In short, harness the power of informational interviews to gain a deeper understanding of your field and to build a valuable network. Remember, the goal is insight, not immediate job offers. With curiosity and professionalism, you'll unlock doors to industry insights that can shape your professional future.

MASTERING NETWORKING EVENTS AND CONFERENCES

The Key Ideas

Embrace a Strategic Mindset

• Understand your goals: Are you there to find job prospects, potential clients, mentors, or collaborators? Knowing this directs your efforts.

• Research attendees and speakers: Prioritize who you want to meet and gather background information to facilitate meaningful conversations.

First Impressions Count

• Dress appropriately: Your attire should match the professional level of the event.

• Perfect your elevator pitch: A concise, impactful introduction is pivotal.

Cultivate Active Listening

• Show genuine interest: Be present during conversations, asking insightful questions and absorbing information.

- Body language matters: Maintain eye contact, nod, and smile to demonstrate engagement.

Practical Implementation

Before the Event

- Preparedness is key:
  - Print business cards.
  - Update your LinkedIn profile.
- Set measurable objectives:
  - Number of people to meet.
  - Specific connections to establish.

At the Event

- Maximize your presence:
  - Arrive early for more interaction opportunities.
  - Volunteer or participate in panels for visibility.

Networking Techniques

- Start conversations with open-ended questions.
- Leverage commonalities to create a rapport.
- Practice the art of remembering names.

Post-Event Follow-Up

- Timely connection: Reach out within 48 hours.

• Personalize your message, reminding them of the interaction.

• Propose a concrete next step, such as a meeting or a phone call.

Consistency and Evaluation

Cultivating Relationships

• Regular contact maintains connections: A brief email or a LinkedIn message can keep the relationship alive.

• Add value to others' networks: Share relevant articles or introductions.

Self-Reflection and Growth

• Post-event analysis: Reflect on what worked and what didn't.

• Feedback is your friend: Don't shy away from asking how you can improve.

Tracking Progress

• Develop a follow-up system: Use a spreadsheet or CRM to monitor relationships.

• Revisit goals periodically and adjust strategies as needed.

BUILDING AND NURTURING YOUR PROFESSIONAL TRIBE

The Key Ideas

Building a professional tribe is about creating a network of colleagues, mentors, and industry connections who provide support, knowledge, and opportunities. It's essential to:

1. **Define Your Tribe**: Understand the kind of professionals who align with your values and industry.

2. **Diversity**: Ensure your tribe represents a range of skills, backgrounds, and perspectives.

3. **Quality Over Quantity**: Focus on deepening relationships rather than collecting contacts.

4. **Mutual Benefit**: Networking is bi-directional; always look for ways to offer value.

5. **Stay Genuine**: Authentic interactions are the foundation of strong professional relationships.

Practical Implementation

Start with these actionable steps:

1. **Identify Key Influencers**: Look for thought leaders in your field and engage with their content.

2. **Engage in Conversation**: Attend industry events, both virtual and in-person, and be a proactive participant.

3. **Leverage Social Media**:

   ○ Follow relevant hashtags and join groups on platforms like LinkedIn.

   ○ Share insightful content and contribute to discussions.

4. **Create Value**: Offer your skills or knowledge in a way that benefits others in your tribe.

5. **Set Up One-to-Ones**: Personal meetings can create stronger bonds than group interactions.

6. **Be Consistent**: Regularly contribute to your tribe with content, insights, and support.

Consistency and Evaluation

To ensure effectiveness:

1. **Regular Check-ins**: Schedule things like coffee chats or progress update emails.

2. **Set Goals**: Have clear objectives for what you want your professional tribe to help you achieve.

3. **Seek Feedback**: Engage with your network to understand what works and what can improve.

4. **Reflect on Relationships**: Annually review each connection to ensure mutual growth.

5. **Adapt Strategies**: Be prepared to pivot networking tactics as your career evolves.

THE ART OF FOLLOW-UP: STAYING ON THE RADAR

The Key Ideas

Strategic follow-up is critical to cementing any professional relationship. After your initial meeting, whatever the environment, pursuing a pertinent and deliberate follow-up strategy ensures that you remain on the radar without irritating or overwhelming the other party.

- **Purposeful Interaction**: Each follow-up should have a clear objective. Whether it's to offer value, seek advice, or further a business relationship, be explicit about your intentions.

- **Timing is Everything**: Strike a balance between persistence and patience. Follow-up too soon, and you might seem desperate; wait too long, and you've become an afterthought.

- **Personalization Wins**: Address the receiver by their name, reference specific points from your last conversation, and tailor your message to their interests or business goals.

- **Value Proposition**: Offer something of value with your follow-up – an article, a relevant introduction, or a solution to a problem they've mentioned.

- **Multichannel Approach**: Use a mix of communication methods – email, phone calls, social media – to stay on the person's radar in a non-intrusive way.

- **Keep it Professional**: Casual language may be appropriate in some industries, but professionalism remains paramount. Respect boundaries and maintain a professional demeanor.

Practical Implementation

Implementing an effective follow-up strategy requires action. Here's how to do it:

1. **Organize Your Contacts**: Categorize them by priority, industry, or the nature of your relationship. Use CRM tools or simple spreadsheets to track interactions and set reminders for follow-ups.

2. **Draft Your Follow-Up Template**: While personalization is key, having a basic structure saves time. Create a template for emails or calls that includes placeholders for customization.

3. **Schedule Your Follow-Ups**: Using your organizational system, decide on optimal timings and set reminders.

4. **Execute with a Touch of Personalization**: Take the extra minute to add a personal note to your template. Make it relevant and sincere.

5. **Add Value**: Attach a piece of content, provide a useful contact, or offer help with a problem. Make your follow-up memorable.

6. **Check for Understanding**: Ensure that your message has been understood as intended. Clarity cannot be compromised.

7. **Acknowledge their Time**: Express appreciation for their time and make it clear you value the relationship.

8. **Review and Iterate**: After each follow-up, take note of the response and tweak your approach if necessary.

Consistency and Evaluation

Every professional relationship is unique, and so should be your follow-up plan. However, maintaining a consistent approach allows for an accurate evaluation.

- **Revisit Goals Regularly**: Every few months, revisit your initial objectives with each contact to ensure your follow-ups align with those goals.

- **Collect Data**: Keep a log of when and how you follow up, the response rate, and the outcome.

- **Review Your Approach**: If a certain method is consistently yielding a low response rate, it's time to change tactics.

- **Seek Feedback**: When appropriate, ask for feedback on your communication style. It provides invaluable insight into how your messages are being received.

Follow these principles to ensure that your follow-up strategy is not only effective but also welcome and anticipated. In networking, it's not just who you know, but how you nurture those connections that matter.

CREATING VALUE: BECOMING A RESOURCE FOR OTHERS

The Key Ideas

To create value in your professional network, you must position yourself as a resource. This means offering tangible benefits, knowledge, and support to others. It's about contributing to their success as you build your own. Real value comes from genuine assistance, not just exchanging business cards or adding contacts on LinkedIn.

- **Identify Needs**: Understand the challenges and objectives of those in your network.

- **Share Expertise**: Offer insights and advice in your area of specialty, showcasing your expertise without being boastful.

- **Connect People**: Act as a connector by introducing individuals who can help each other.

- **Provide Resources**: Share articles, case studies, tools, or even mentorship that can aid others.

- **Follow Through**: When you promise assistance, deliver on that promise promptly.

Practical Implementation

To become a resource, it's critical to practice certain behaviors consistently:

1. **Listen Actively**: Pay close attention to what others say. This attentiveness will help you identify how you can be of service.

2. **Inquire**: Ask questions to deepen your understanding of what others are seeking.

3. **Stay Informed**: Keep up with industry trends and news. Be ready to offer relevant and current information.

4. **Leverage Your Network**: Use your contacts to create opportunities not just for yourself but also for others. This reciprocity will often come back to benefit you.

Be patient. Building trust and demonstrating value takes time, but the investment often leads to stronger, more meaningful connections.

Consistency and Evaluation

Maintaining a consistent approach in offering value requires periodic assessment:

- **Review Your Contributions**: Reflect on what you've offered and how it has been received.

- **Seek Feedback**: Ask for input from those you've helped. Use this information to refine your approach.

- **Set Goals**: Aim for specific networking milestones, like making a certain number of intros each month.

- **Adapt**: Networking landscapes change. Be willing to evolve your methods of providing value.

Remember: Your worth to your network is not just in what you provide but in your reliability as a source of assistance. Stand out as an invaluable node in your professional web by consistently being a resource to others.

NETWORKING IN DIVERSE CULTURAL CONTEXTS

The Key Ideas

Networking across various cultural landscapes calls for both adaptability and sensitivity. Key considerations include:

- **Awareness of Cultural Norms:** Every culture has its own set of unwritten rules. Before engaging, learn these norms to avoid missteps.

- **Communication Styles:** Direct and indirect communication can vary widely. Tailor your approach to align with the cultural expectations.

- **Language Barriers:** Clear and simplified language helps bridge gaps. Patience and paraphrasing are tools, not crutches.

- **Listening Skills:** Listening is universal. Demonstrate respect and understanding by actively listening more than you speak.

- **Adaptability:** Cultures are dynamic. Stay informed and ready to adjust your behavior as necessary.

- **Inclusivity:** Embrace diversity in your network. Include individuals with varied backgrounds and experiences.

Practical Implementation

Laying out steps for networking within diverse cultural contexts involves targeted actions:

1. **Research and Learn:** Dive deep into the culture where you wish to network. Understand history, customs, and etiquette.

2. **Mind the Language:** Choose your words wisely, limiting jargon and colloquialisms. Consider a language course if the situation merits.

3. **Seek First to Understand:** Start conversations by learning about the other party. Their cultural perspective is a gateway to effective communication.

4. **Find Common Ground:** Identify shared interests or goals as a foundation for developing the relationship.

5. **Follow Local Norms:** Adapt your behavior based on what you've learned, whether it's exchanging business cards in Japan or engaging in small talk in Brazil.

6. **Ask and Reflect:** Don't assume. Ask questions to clarify and show interest in learning and understand the value of reflection on interactions.

7. **Develop Cultural Intelligence (CQ):** Work on the capability to relate and work effectively across cultures. This includes motivation, cognition, and behavior.

8. **Network Virtually and In-Person:** Utilize technology to bridge distances, but also value face-to-face interactions when possible.

Consistency and Evaluation

To network effectively in diverse cultures, consistently evaluate and refine your approach:

- **Track Progress**: Regularly review your networking outcomes. Adjust strategies as you gain more cultural insights.

- **Solicit Feedback**: Ask for direct input from cultural insiders. What could you have done differently? What worked well?

- **Self-Reflect**: Consider your own biases and how they may impact your networking. Continuously strive to expand your cultural understanding.

- **Build Long-Term Relationships**: Networking isn't just a one-off. Commit to nurturing the connections you make, respecting cultural dynamics along the way.

- **Measure Success**: Define what success looks like in each cultural context. It may vary, but should always include mutual benefit and understanding.

In summary, networking across cultural lines is enriching and requires a dedicated approach. Embrace learning, remain authentic, and adapt as necessary to form meaningful professional relationships.

OVERCOMING SHYNESS AND NETWORKING WITH CONFIDENCE

The Key Ideas

Networking is a Skill: Like any skill, networking can be improved with practice. If shyness prevents you from networking effectively, recognize that confidence can be developed over time.

Build Your Foundation: Before stepping into a networking situation, understand your strengths and what you bring to the table. This gives you a base of confidence to rely on.

Reframe Your Mindset: Shift away from seeing networking as a series of transactions and view it as an opportunity to build genuine relationships and learn from others.

Small Steps Lead to Big Changes: Start with smaller, less intimidating networking scenarios and gradually increase the challenge as you build confidence.

Prepare and Practice: Have a set of questions and topics ready for discussion. Practice conversations with friends or in front of a mirror.

Practical Implementation

1. **Set Realistic Goals:** Begin by setting achievable networking goals, such as talking to two new people at an event.

2. **Create an Elevator Pitch:** Develop a short summary about yourself and what you do, to succinctly introduce yourself when opportunities arise.

3. **Choose the Right Environment:** Pick networking events that align with your interests to ensure a level of comfort and common ground.

4. **Use Body Language to Your Advantage:** Practice open body language, solid eye contact, and a firm handshake to project confidence.

5. **Leverage Social Media:** Start online to initiate connections that can later transition into in-person relationships.

6. **Find a Networking Buddy:** Partner with a friend or colleague who is more experienced in networking to help guide you through the process.

7. **Celebrate Small Victories:** Acknowledge your progress, no matter how small, to build momentum.

Consistency and Evaluation

Tracking Your Progress: Keep a record of each networking event you attend, whom you meet, and follow up on connections. Notice patterns in what strategies work best for you.

Evaluating Success: Don't just measure success by the number of contacts you make but by the quality of the relationships you build and how they contribute to your professional development.

Continuous Learning: Reflect on your networking experiences, both positive and negative, to constantly refine your approach.

Seek Feedback: Ask trusted contacts for their impression of your networking style and for suggestions on improvement.

Remember, networking is a marathon, not a sprint. It's about cultivating relationships over time, not just collecting business cards. Stay true to yourself, and your authenticity will resonate with others. It's not about being the most outgoing person in the room – it's about being genuine, prepared, and open to connecting.

COLD CONNECTIONS: REACHING OUT TO NEW CONTACTS

The Key Ideas

Networking is an art – one that entails building relationships, not just exchanging business cards. Approaching new contacts with care and sincerity is crucial.

- **Research**: Before reaching out, know your contact. Understand their work, values, and interests.

- **Personalization is Key**: Generic messages are lackluster. Tailor your communication to show genuine interest.

- **Value Proposition**: Offer something of value. It could be insight, assistance, or relevant information.

- **Mutual Benefits**: Aim for a connection that brings mutual gains, however small.

- **First Impressions Matter**: Professionalism and clarity in your initial message can set the tone for the relationship.

Practical Implementation

1. **Identify Potential Contacts**: Use LinkedIn, industry events, and publications to find individuals aligning with your professional goals.

2. **Engage Subtly**: Comment on their posts, or mention their work in your circles, building a soft introduction.

3. **Craft Compelling Messages**:

   - Subject Line: Grab attention with clarity and relevance.

   - Clearly state who you are and why you're reaching out.

   - Connection Point: Reference a shared interest or contact.

   - Value Offer: Quickly articulate what you can offer them.

   - Call to Action: Propose a clear, specific, and easy step for follow-up.

4. **Follow Up, But Don't Nag**: If there's no response, follow up in a week or two with a brief reminder. Respect their time and decision if they're not interested.

5. **Track and Organize Contacts**: Use a CRM tool or a spreadsheet to keep track of communications and follow-ups.

Consistency and Evaluation

Consistency – Preserve the integrity of your networking efforts by regularly reaching out to new contacts and nurturing existing relationships.

- Schedule time each week for networking activities.

- Reflect on connections made, and note any responses or lack thereof.

• Stay active within professional communities.

Evaluation – Regularly assess your networking strategies. What's working? What isn't? Revise your methods based on your experiences and the outcomes.

• Track response rates to your outreach efforts.

• Seek feedback where possible.

• Adjust your approach based on the industry climate and individual preferences.

Remember, cold connections can blossom into prosperous professional relationships with a thoughtful and dedicated approach.

MAINTAINING LONG-TERM PROFESSIONAL RELATIONSHIPS

The Key Ideas

In the realm of professional networking, longevity of relationships is crucial. People tend to focus on initial connections but often neglect the continuous nurturing required. Think of professional relationships like a garden; they need regular care and attention to flourish. Here are the key ideas to maintain these relationships effectively:

• **Mutual Benefit**: Strong relationships hinge on reciprocal value. Seek ways to assist others, and be open to their support in return.

• **Consistent Communication**: Stay in touch, but avoid overwhelming your contacts. Strive for a balance between presence and respect for their time.

• **Personal Touch**: Remember details like birthdays, important events, or career milestones. Small gestures can have a big impact.

• **Adaptability**: People and circumstances change. Be willing to adapt the nature of your connections over time.

• **Respect Boundaries**: Professionalism is paramount. Always respect personal and professional boundaries.

• **Genuine Interest**: Show sincere interest in your contacts' welfare and achievements. Authenticity fosters trust.

• **Reputation Management**: Your personal brand is a reflection on those you associate with. Maintain a reputation that others are proud to be connected with.

Practical Implementation

Implementing these key ideas does not require grand gestures, but rather a series of small, consistent actions:

1. **Set Reminders**: Use digital tools to prompt regular check-ins.

2. **Professional Groups**: Join forums or groups that your contacts frequent. Engage with the community.

3. **Mentor and Seek Mentorship**: Share knowledge and expertise, and be receptive to learning from others.

4. **Offer Help Before You Need It**: Offer your skills and resources without immediate expectation of return.

5. **Follow Up**: After meetings or conversations, send a thank-you note or a message reflecting on the discussion.

6. **Networking Events**: Attend events where you can interact with your contacts in person.

Consistency and Evaluation

Consistency

• Keep a calendar of networking activities.

- Dedicate a certain time each week or month for relationship upkeep.

- Stay informed about your industry to remain a relevant contact.

Evaluation

- Periodically assess the health of your professional relationships.

- Are they mutually beneficial? Is there balanced give-and-take?

- Adapt your strategies based on what works and what doesn't.

In conclusion, long-term professional relationships require deliberate effort and strategic thinking. By implementing these practices, you'll build a network that not only survives but thrives over time.

COLLABORATION: NETWORKING WITH PEERS VERSUS SUPERIORS

The Key Ideas

Networking, a vital skill in your professional arsenal, encapsulates a spectrum of relationships, prominently with peers and superiors. Mastering the art of networking horizontally with your contemporary colleagues and vertically with your higher-ups unlocks doors for collaborative opportunities, insight exchange, and career progression.

Networking with Peers: The bedrock of trust and mutual support. Your peers often become your sounding board for new ideas and your partners in executing projects. Highlighting these key ideas:

- Share and exchange skills and knowledge

- Offer and solicit feedback comfortably

- Develop long-term professional relationships

Networking with Superiors: Vital for mentorship and growth. This networking lane is integral for gaining strategic insights, garnering support for upward mobility, and understanding the higher-level decision-making process. To emphasize:

- Seek guidance and advice

- Understand broader organizational goals

- Establish visibility and credibility

Practical Implementation

1. **Start with Mutual Interests**: Identify common professional interests with peers and superiors. Apex points for conversation build rapport and facilitate ongoing communication.

2. **Engagement through Projects or Committees**: Volunteer for cross-departmental projects or committees to broaden your network. Interdisciplinary initiatives ripple with wide-spreading networking effects.

3. **Host or Attend Networking Events**: Organize or participate in inter-office mixers or industry conferences. Face-to-face interaction cements the foundation for solid professional relationships.

4. **Mentorship Programs**: Opt into mentorship opportunities. If unavailable, propose a mentorship program. A structured framework for superior-peer interaction accelerates professional development.

5. **Knowledge Sharing Sessions**: Create regular team meetings or 'lunch and learns' to present thought leadership and industry trends. Encourage peers and superiors alike to contribute, fostering a culture of learning and collaboration.

Consistency and Evaluation

- **Establish Regular Check-Ins**: Scheduled meetings with peers and superiors ensure continuous dialogue and reliable presence.

• **Feedback Loops**: Create mechanisms for regular feedback, ensuring reciprocal growth and the nurturing of genuine relationships.

• **Set Networking Goals**: Define clear, measurable objectives for networking efforts. Aim for quality interactions over quantity.

• **Review and Adjust**: Bi-annual reviews of your networking activities help you gauge effectiveness and pivot strategies where necessary.

• **Document Success Stories**: Record instances where networking has directly benefitted a project or your career. Acknowledge collaborative wins.

Networking is a dynamic and reciprocal journey. Whether paddling in the peer pond or navigating the superior stream, the essence remains in authentic connection and purposeful engagement. In the ecosystem of career growth, your ability to adeptly network, both laterally and vertically, differentiates you as a proactive and thoughtful professional, poised for success.

NETWORKING AND THOUGHT LEADERSHIP: ESTABLISHING YOUR EXPERTISE

The Key Ideas

• Being seen as a thought leader is a powerful way to build your professional network.

• Share unique insights and offer valuable perspectives on industry trends and challenges.

• Become actively involved in professional communities to enhance your visibility and credibility.

• Use digital platforms to demonstrate your expertise and contribute to wider conversations.

Practical Implementation

1. **Identify your niche**: Pinpoint the area within your industry where you can offer the greatest insight and value. Consider what topics you are passionate about and where you see a knowledge gap that you can fill.

2. **Build a content strategy**:

   ○ Start a blog to regularly share your knowledge.

- Use LinkedIn to publish articles and engage with other professionals.

    - Consider starting a podcast or a webinar series.

    - Speak at industry conferences and participate in panel discussions.

3. **Engage with the community**:

    - Comment on relevant articles and posts.

    - Join professional groups online and offline.

    - Answer questions in forums like Quora or specialized industry platforms.

4. **Leverage Social Media**:

    - Tweet regularly about industry news.

    - Share your content and other relevant articles on your social media channels.

    - Interact with industry influencers and your followers.

5. **Continuous Learning**:

    - Stay updated with the latest industry trends and news.

    - Enroll in courses and pursue certifications.

    - Read widely within and outside your field to connect the dots and bring new perspectives.

Consistency and Evaluation

- **Set a publishing schedule**: Regularly releasing content helps maintain visibility and encourages sustained engagement with your network.

- **Track your progress**: Use analytics tools to measure engagement with your posts, articles, and other content. Adjust your strategy based on what resonates with your audience.

- **Solicit feedback**: Encourage commentary on your work and be open to constructive criticism.

- **Self-reflect**: Regularly assess whether your efforts are enhancing your reputation as a thought leader and expanding your network.

A strong network isn't built overnight, and neither is a reputation for thought leadership. By consistently providing value in your chosen niche and engaging others, you establish not just expertise, but trust—and from trust comes the most valuable professional relationships.

CROSS-INDUSTRY NETWORKING: EXPANDING YOUR CIRCLE

The Key Ideas

Defining Cross-Industry Networking Cross-Industry Networking is the strategic practice of building professional relationships across various sectors, not just your own. It's about connecting the dots between different industries to leverage diverse perspectives, skills, and opportunities.

- **Why Go Cross-Industry**

  - **Innovation**: Exposure to different industry practices can inspire new ideas.

  - **Resilience**: Diverse connections can offer stability in a fast-paced economy.

  - **Opportunities**: Access to broader career and business opportunities.

Benefits of Varied Perspectives Curating a rich, diverse network can lead to innovative problem-solving, as cross-industry insights inspire breakthroughs that may be unheard of in your primary field.

- **Think Differently**: Cross-pollinate ideas and challenge industry norms.

- **Skill Enhancement**: Learn skills not yet prevalent in your own sector.

Cross-Industry Event Targeting Identify and attend events not typically frequented by your industry peers to foster unique connections.

- **Conferences**: From tech expos to design symposiums.

- **Seminars/Webinars**: Expand knowledge and networks simultaneously.

- **Trade Shows**: Find the intersections between your work and others.

Practical Implementation

Building Bridges Begin with industries related to your own and gradually branch out. Find common ground where interests and objectives intersect.

- **Research**: Use platforms like LinkedIn to find industry leaders.

- **Introductions**: A mutual connection can introduce you to their cross-industry contacts.

Leverage Social Media Social media platforms are fertile ground for cross-industry connections. Engage with content from various sectors to make your interest and presence known.

- **Follow Thought Leaders**: From different industries on Twitter or LinkedIn.

- **Join Groups**: Engage in conversations in industry-specific LinkedIn or Facebook groups.

- **Content Sharing**: Share and comment on content beyond your field.

Networking Strategies

- **Set Goals**: Define what you wish to achieve from these interactions.

- **Elevator Pitch**: Prepare a concise introduction that resonates across industries.

- **Active Listening**: Show genuine interest in their work, which encourages reciprocal attention.

Consistency and Evaluation

Follow-Up Post-meeting, connect on LinkedIn with a personalized message. Nurture the relationship by checking in periodically and sharing relevant information.

Consistency is Key Regularly attend cross-industry events and maintain an active social media presence. You must put in consistent effort to reap the benefits of a diverse network.

Measure Progress

- **Network Growth**: Assess the number of new connections made.

- **Quality Interactions**: The depth and potential of relationships matter.

- **Opportunities Emerged**: Monitor the direct and indirect opportunities from these connections.

Evaluate and Adjust Ask for feedback, reflect on strategies that work, and always be ready to refine your approach to better suit your evolving networking goals.

Remember, cross-industry networking isn't about collecting contacts; it's about cultivating meaningful, diverse professional relationships that broaden your horizons and create mutual value.

TURNING NETWORKING INTO COLLABORATIVE OPPORTUNITIES

The Key Ideas

Networking isn't merely about exchanging business cards; it's about building a web of mutually beneficial relationships. Delve into these core principles that make the difference:

- **Value Exchange**: Understand that networking is a two-way street. Anticipate not only what you need but also what you can offer. It's about creating a balance where both parties see the benefit of working together.

- **Common Goals**: Align with individuals and organizations that share similar objectives. This synergy often spawns the best collaborative opportunities.

- **Trust and Rapport**: Strong collaborations are built on trust. Spend time nurturing relationships before expecting to collaborate.

- **Active Listening**: Pay attention to the needs and challenges of others. By actively listening, you position yourself to offer meaningful contributions.

• **Quality Over Quantity**: Focus on deepening a few key relationships rather than amassing a large number of superficial connections.

Practical Implementation

1. **Identify Prospects**:

   ○ List potential collaborators who share your interests or goals.

   ○ Research their current projects or problems they might be facing.

2. **Prepare Your Offer**:

   ○ Clearly define what you bring to the table.

   ○ Create a value proposition that is hard to ignore.

3. **Engage with Authenticity**:

   ○ Initiate contact with a personal touch. Avoid templates or generic messages.

   ○ Be genuine in your communication, reflecting your real interest in their work.

4. **Follow-Up Effectively**:

   ○ If there's no immediate response, follow up with a gentle reminder.

   ○ Provide additional information that might pique their interest.

5. **Seal the Collaboration**:

   ○ Once interest is mutual, propose a concrete plan for collaboration.

- Discuss and agree upon roles, responsibilities, and outcomes.

6. **Foster the Relationship**:

   - Keep the communication alive even after a project is complete.

   - Check in periodically, share relevant information, and be a resource.

Consistency and Evaluation

- **Set Networking Goals**: Establish regular objectives for your networking efforts. Aim to identify a specific number of potential collaborators each month.

- **Track Progress**: Keep a record of your interactions and evaluate which strategies yield the best results.

- **Reflect and Adjust**: Regularly analyze the outcomes of your networking activities. Identify what works and where there's room for improvement.

- **Stay Proactive**: Consistently look for new opportunities and don't be afraid to reach out.

- **Assess Collaborations**: After each project or engagement, evaluate the success of the collaboration. Did it meet the initial goals? What lessons were learned?

In optimizing networking for collaborative opportunities, remember the hallmarks of success are value creation, shared objectives, and long-term relationships. By following these guidelines, you can transform casual connections into powerful partnerships.

THE ALTRUISTIC NETWORKER: HELPING OTHERS SUCCEED

The Key Ideas

You know the basics of networking: it's not just about what you can get, but what you can give. We explore a shift in perspective—placing others' needs and successes before your own can lead to more fruitful relationships and, in turn, your own success. Here are the core principles:

- Lead with generosity: Proffer assistance before seeking it.

- Cultivate genuine relationships: Interests align naturally when you foster sincere connections.

- Share knowledge freely: Your expertise can pave the way for others.

- Facilitate introductions: Connect contacts who could benefit from knowing each other.

- Celebrate others' achievements: Show your support openly and enthusiastically.

Practical Implementation

These ideas are actionable. Below is how you can integrate them into your networking endeavors:

Offer Assistance Without Expectation

When meeting new connections or catching up with existing ones, inquire about their current projects and offer your help, whether it's your time, advice, or resources.

Listen More Than You Talk

Active listening shows you value others' contributions, leading to stronger, more altruistic connections. This approach helps you understand their needs better.

Share Opportunities

If an opportunity isn't right for you but could benefit someone else, pass it along. This reinforces trust and goodwill.

Introduce Colleagues

If two people in your network could benefit from knowing each other, make the introduction. Provide context and why you think they should meet.

Publicly Praise and Endorse

Use platforms like LinkedIn to endorse skills and congratulate your connections on their achievements. Public recognition goes a long way.

Consistency and Evaluation

Maintain the following practices to ensure your altruistic networking is both consistent and effective:

Regular Check-ins

Schedule periodic meetings or touchpoints with your connections to offer continued support and stay updated on their endeavors.

Track Contributions

Keep a personal log of your assistance to others. Reflect on the outcomes, both for them and for any indirect benefits to your career.

Request Feedback

Ask your connections about the value you've provided. Their insights can guide your future networking efforts.

Adapt and Evolve

As you gather feedback, tailor your approach. Relationships grow —what worked once might need refining.

Altruistic networking is an art form, requiring balance, sincerity, and active engagement. When done right, it turns your network into a community of mutual success.

BUILDING A NETWORKING STRATEGY FOR CAREER TRANSITIONS

The Key Ideas

Your network is a dynamic resource that evolves with your career. It is not just a list of contacts but a map that guides you through career transitions. Understanding how to leverage this map is imperative, especially when navigating the uncertain terrain of a career change. Here are the key ideas for building an effective networking strategy during these transitions:

- **Identify Transition Goals**: Clarify why you're transitioning and what you aim to achieve. Your goals guide your networking direction.

- **Research and Reach Out**: Investigate your desired field, and connect with industry insiders. Aim for informational interviews to gain insights.

- **Adjust Your Value Proposition**: Tailor your introduction and capabilities to resonate with your new industry's needs.

- **Cultivate Champions**: Seek mentors and influencers who can open doors and advocate for you.

- **Strategic Visibility**: Increase your visibility in your desired field through conferences, social media, and articles.

Practical Implementation

To successfully implement your networking strategy, you need to take concrete steps. Here's how to break down your strategy into actionable tasks:

1. **Goal Setting**: Write down your career transition objectives. Use these goals to determine the types of connections you need to make.

2. **Mapping Your Network**: List current contacts that could be relevant to your transition. Identify gaps and who you need to meet to bridge them.

3. **Communication Plan**: Craft messages tailored to different types of contacts—peers, mentors, industry leaders. Explain your career shift and express genuine interest in their expertise.

4. **Leverage Social Platforms**: Update your LinkedIn profile to reflect your transition. Join relevant groups and participate in discussions.

5. **Regularly Attend Industry Events**: Conferences and webinars offer rich opportunities to meet new contacts and learn about industry trends.

6. **Follow-Up**: Establish a routine for following up with new connections. A simple message recalling your conversation can be effective.

7. **Offer Value**: Networking is reciprocal. Share articles, introduce connections, or offer your skills as ways to bring value to your network.

Consistency and Evaluation

A robust networking strategy demands regular attention and evaluation. Here's how to maintain momentum and assess your progress:

- **Consistency**: Dedicate time each week to network-building activities. This rhythmic commitment solidifies habits and keeps you at the forefront of your contacts' minds.

- **Track Interactions**: Keep a record of who you meet and key takeaways from each interaction. Set reminders for follow-ups.

- **Seek Feedback**: Request feedback from new contacts about your approach. Use this insight to refine your strategy.

- **Measure Progress**: Every month, review your networking activities against your transition goals. Consider both quantitative (e.g., number of new contacts) and qualitative (e.g., depth of relationships) metrics.

- **Adjust as Needed**: Be flexible and ready to shift your strategy if you're not making the desired progress. Networking strategies should evolve with your career journey.

In lesson, build a tailored networking strategy, implement it with tangible actions, stay consistent in your efforts, and regularly evaluate your success. This chapter arms you with a practical approach to navigate your career transition with confidence, fueled by a formidable network.

LEVERAGING ALUMNI NETWORKS FOR PROFESSIONAL SUCCESS

The Key Ideas

Relationships Matter: At its core, an alumni network is a community built on shared experiences. The bond of attending the same institution gives you a common ground with thousands, perhaps millions, of individuals.

Resources at Your Fingertips: Most alumni networks offer directories, events, and platforms to help you connect. This infrastructure is a treasure trove for those who are keen to reach out and engage with fellow alumni.

Mutual Benefit: Remember, networking isn't just about what you can take, but also about what you can offer. Approach your alumni network with a mindset of mutual growth and assistance.

Long-Term Investment: Building connections through an alumni network is a long-term investment. Cultivate these relationships before you need them so that when the time comes, you have a robust support system.

Practical Implementation

1. **Register and Engage**:

   - Sign up for alumni directories and newsletters to stay informed.

   - Attend reunions, chapter meetings, and virtual events.

   - Engage with alumni content on social media platforms.

2. **Make Personal Connections**:

   - Reach out to fellow alumni individually, whether to congratulate them on a career milestone or to inquire about industry insights.

   - Stay genuine. Tailor your communication rather than sending generic messages.

3. **Contribute**:

   - Offer your skills and insights. It could be mentoring fresh graduates or speaking at an event.

   - Share opportunities like job openings or collaborative projects.

4. **Utilize Career Resources**:

   - Take advantage of career coaching, workshops, or webinars offered to alumni.

   - Review job boards and career services that might be exclusive to your alumni network.

5. **Stay Updated**:

   - Keep your own alumni profile updated with your latest professional achievements and contact information.

- Regularly check the network's portals to stay abreast of news and opportunities.

Consistency and Evaluation

Action Plan:

- Schedule regular check-ins with your network, perhaps monthly or quarterly.

- Set goals for networking, such as making a certain number of connections each year.

Measuring Impact:

- Keep track of the outcomes. Did an interaction lead to a job offer, valuable advice, or a partnership?

- Periodically assess if the time spent on networking activities aligns with your professional growth.

Adjust as Needed:

- Be flexible with your strategies. If certain actions do not yield results, pivot and try new approaches.

- Stay informed on the best practices in networking, and continually refine your methods.

Networking through alumni channels can open doors to untapped opportunities. Approach the process with a spirit of authenticity, consistency, and eagerness to both learn and contribute. This strategic investment of your time and energy will construct a meaningful web of professional relationships poised to accelerate your success.

THE DYNAMICS OF INTERNAL COMPANY NETWORKING

The Key Ideas

Internal networking within a company fosters a culture of connectivity, collaboration, and mutual support that can drive success. It's a web of relationships among colleagues at all levels that can lead to new opportunities, knowledge exchange, and innovative ideas. Through intentional networking, you can build these essential connections.

• **Relationship Building Over Transactions**: Networking is about cultivating long-term relationships, not just short-term gains. Focus on how you can help others rather than what you can get from them.

• **Diverse Connections Matter**: Seek connections beyond your immediate team. Interacting with people from different departments can provide new perspectives and insights.

• **Visibility and Engagement Are Key**: Actively participate in company events and online forums; visibility can pave the way for networking opportunities.

• **Mutual Benefit is Essential**: Always consider how the relationship can be mutually beneficial. Networking is a two-way street.

Practical Implementation

To implement effective internal networking, you should take a strategic approach:

1. **Assess your current network**: Determine who you know, how well you know them, and how you can further cultivate those relationships.

2. **Set networking goals**: Define what you want to achieve through your networking efforts. This might include learning new skills or gaining allies for future projects.

3. **Get involved in company initiatives**: Volunteer for projects or committees that align with your goals. This raises your profile and brings you into contact with people who share your interests.

4. **Use company platforms**: Leverage internal messaging boards, social networks, or intranets to showcase your expertise and to engage with colleagues.

5. **Create or join a networking group**: Start a special interest group within your company or join an existing one to meet like-minded colleagues.

6. **Schedule informational interviews**: These can be an excellent way to learn about other roles in the company and show your interest in professional growth.

Consistency and Evaluation

Staying committed to networking is crucial. It's an ongoing process, not a one-time event.

- **Regular Check-ins**: Schedule regular intervals to evaluate your network's health. Are you maintaining relationships? Are you adding new contacts regularly?

• **Re-evaluate Goals**: As your career evolves, so should your networking goals. Adjust them as necessary to align with your professional objectives.

• **Feedback is Invaluable**: Seek feedback from your contacts about your interactions. This will provide insight into how you're perceived and where you can improve.

To conclude, internal company networking demands commitment, strategy, and adaptability. By following the outlined strategies and consistently evaluating your progress, you'll maximize the potential of your professional ecosystem.

Remember, it's the quality of connections, not just the quantity, that can truly accelerate your career.

MASTERING NON-VERBAL COMMUNICATION IN NETWORKING

The Key Ideas

Understanding non-verbal communication is crucial for effective networking. This "silent language" can convey confidence, interest, and trustworthiness, or conversely, disinterest and dishonesty. Non-verbal cues are composed of body language, facial expressions, gestures, eye contact, posture, and even your appearance. Mastering these elements can enhance your networking experience, allowing you to connect with others more profoundly and positively.

- **Body Language**: Your stance and movements send powerful signals. A firm stance conveys confidence, while slouching can suggest disinterest or lack of confidence.

- **Facial Expressions**: Smiling indicates openness and approachability. Maintaining a neutral or pleasant expression is key during conversations.

- **Gestures**: Controlled gestures can emphasize points and express enthusiasm, but avoid fidgeting or aggressive movements.

- **Eye Contact**: Appropriate eye contact signifies engagement and sincerity but be mindful not to stare, which can be perceived as aggressive.

- **Posture**: Stand or sit up straight to denote attentiveness and enthusiasm. Relaxed shoulders suggest comfort and ease in the interaction.

- **Appearance**: Dressing appropriately for the occasion shows respect and attention to detail.

Practical Implementation

To apply these key ideas in a networking setting, follow these actionable steps:

1. **Observe and Mirror**: Take note of the body language of effective communicators. Practice mimicking these positive signals to improve your own non-verbal communication.

2. **Self-Awareness**: Frequently check in on your own body language. Adjust your posture, relax your face, and make appropriate gestures that align with your verbal messages.

3. **Feedback Loops**: Ask trusted peers or mentors for feedback on your non-verbal cues. Are you coming off as intended?

4. **Practice Sessions**: Rehearse introductions and conversations with a focus on non-verbal aspects. Record yourself to identify areas for improvement.

5. **Real-Time Adjustments**: Be ready to adjust your non-verbal cues in real-time based on the reactions of those you are engaging with. Lack of interest or discomfort suggests a need to change tack.

Consistency and Evaluation

Consistent application and regular evaluation of your non-verbal communication will yield the best results. Maintain authenticity—align your non-verbals with your spoken words. Fake signals are often easily spotted and can undermine trust.

- **Regular Check-ins**: Schedule moments, post-networking events, to reflect on your non-verbal performance. What worked well? What could be improved?

- **Continuous Improvement**: Make adjustments based on reflections and feedback. Set specific goals for each networking opportunity.

- **Benchmarking Success**: Define what successful non-verbal communication means to you—be it making a certain number of new contacts or achieving a specific level of engagement during conversations.

In conclusion, non-verbal communication is a silent yet eloquent partner to your spoken words in networking. By mastering this art, you are poised to make more meaningful connections that can have a lasting impact on your professional journey.

THE IMPORTANCE OF A DIVERSE NETWORK

The Key Ideas

In today's professional landscape, the power of networking cannot be overstated. However, the strength of a network is not just in its size, but its diversity. A diverse network offers a wider array of perspectives, opportunities, and resources. Here are the critical points that illuminate why diversity in your network is crucial:

- **Broader Perspectives**: Engage with people from different industries, backgrounds, and cultures to enrich your worldview.

- **Increased Opportunities**: A varied network opens doors in various sectors, amplifying career prospects.

- **Innovation and Creativity**: Cross-pollination of ideas from various fields can lead to innovative solutions.

- **Learning and Growth**: Interacting with a diverse group allows for continuous learning and personal development.

- **Resilience**: A heterogeneous network can provide support and solutions during industry-specific downturns.

Practical Implementation

Building a diverse network demands intentional actions:

1. **Attend Varied Networking Events**: Step out of your comfort zone and attend events outside of your industry.

2. **Volunteer**: Offer your skills to different organizations to meet people from various walks of life.

3. **Join Cross-Discipline Groups**: Be a part of groups that are not directly related to your field.

4. **Connect Online**: Use professional social media platforms to connect with diverse professionals.

5. **Cultivate a Curious Mindset**: Approach every conversation as a learning opportunity.

When engaging with your network:

- **Be Genuine**: Forge connections based on real interest and respect.

- **Offer Value**: Always think of how you can help others in your network.

- **Listen**: Actively listen to understand the experiences and views of others.

Consistency and Evaluation

A diverse network doesn't grow overnight, it requires commitment:

- **Set Networking Goals**: Define what diversity means to you and identify specific diversity goals in your networking strategy.

• **Schedule Regular Check-ins**: Frequently reassess your network to ensure that you're not drifting back into a homogenous professional circle.

• **Solicit Feedback**: Ask for honest feedback about your networking style and adapt accordingly.

• **Measure Success Through Outcomes**: Evaluate the benefits that your diverse network has provided to your career and personal growth.

Remember, the true merit of a diverse network is not in numbers but in the richness of relationships and the multitude of perspectives it brings to your professional life. Keeping these principles in practice, you can build and maintain a network that not only propels your career forward but also contributes significantly to your personal development.

TAILORING YOUR NETWORKING APPROACH TO DIFFERENT AUDIENCES

The Key Ideas

- **Understand Your Audience**: Know the interests, challenges, and language of the groups you're networking with. Research before engaging.

- **Adapt Your Message**: Fine-tune your introduction, pitch, and conversation topics to resonate with the specific audience.

- **Cultural Sensitivity**: Be aware of and respect cultural differences that may influence communication styles and preferences.

- **Active Listening**: Show genuine interest in understanding others' perspectives and responding thoughtfully.

Practical Implementation

1. **Research**:

   - Investigate the industry, company cultures, and individual backgrounds.

   - Use LinkedIn, industry publications, and event descriptions to gather insights.

2. **Goal-setting**:

- Define what you intend to achieve from each networking interaction.

- Set clear objectives like forming partnerships, learning, or sharing knowledge.

3. **Elevator Pitch Variation**:

- Create different versions of your elevator pitch to cater to distinct audiences.

- Highlight relevant experiences or interests that align with the individual or group.

4. **Question Arsenal**:

- Prepare a set of open-ended questions tailored to learn more about your audience.

- Questions should invite discussion and not just simple yes/no answers.

5. **Adapt Your Presence**:

- Modify your tone, body language, and energy to match the setting and audience.

- Be more reserved in formal settings and conversational in casual environments.

6. **Follow-Up Personalization**:

- Send follow-up messages that reference specific topics discussed.

- Show appreciation for the time spent and any insights shared.

7. **Audience Feedback**:

   ◦ After your interaction, seek feedback to understand how your approach was received.

   ◦ Use this to refine your technique for future encounters.

Consistency and Evaluation

• **Regular Review**: Evaluate your networking approach with each audience periodically.

• **Consistency in Values**: While your approach may change, your core values and authenticity should remain constant.

• **Outcome Assessment**:

   ◦ Reflect on the success of your interactions and the growth of your network.

   ◦ Consider both quantity (number of new connections) and quality (depth of relationships).

• **Continuous Learning**:

   ◦ Keep abreast of changing communication trends and audience expectations.

   ◦ Refine your approach based on new learnings and feedback.

In networking, it's not one-size-fits-all. Recognize and embrace the diversity of your professional landscape. As you tailor your approach to different audiences, you'll cultivate a rich, multifaceted network grounded in mutual respect and genuine connection.

EFFECTIVE NETWORKING FOR ENTREPRENEURS AND STARTUPS

The Key Ideas

Networking is an essential stride for entrepreneurs and startups. It opens doors to new opportunities, resources, and knowledge. Here are the key ideas you should be focusing on:

- Build genuine relationships rather than just contacts.

- Value quality over quantity in your network.

- Tailor your approach depending on the context and person.

- Offer value before expecting anything in return.

- Utilize online platforms and in-person events strategically.

- Maintain a diverse network across various industries and roles.

Networking is not just exchanging business cards; it's about fostering authentic connections that can mutually benefit all parties involved.

Practical Implementation

To put the key ideas into action, engage with the following actionable steps:

Getting Started

1. **Identify Your Goals**: Define what you hope to achieve through networking. It could be finding investors, partners, or advisors.

2. **Research Events and Platforms**: Locate events such as conferences, meetups, and workshops. Also identify online platforms relevant to your field.

3. **Prepare an Elevator Pitch**: Craft a concise pitch summarizing who you are, what you do, and what you're looking for.

4. **Use Social Media Wisely**: Create professional profiles on platforms like LinkedIn, and engage with relevant content to increase visibility.

Building and Maintaining Your Network

- **Initiating Conversations**: Start with a question or a compliment. Make your first interaction about the other person, not yourself.

- **Follow-Up**: After meeting someone, send a personalized message recalling your conversation and expressing interest in staying in touch.

- **Organize Your Contacts**: Maintain a database of your network contacts, noting relevant information and follow-ups.

- **Nurture Relationships**: Regularly touch base with your connections. Share updates, congratulate them on achievements, or send articles of interest.

Providing Value

- **Be a Connector**: Introduce people in your network who could benefit from knowing each other.

- **Offer Your Expertise**: Share your knowledge with your network or help solve problems without expecting immediate returns.

- **Stay Visible and Valuable**: Publish thought leadership articles, participate in panel discussions, or host webinars.

Consistency and Evaluation

The effectiveness of your networking efforts relies on consistency and regular evaluation. Here's how to maintain that:

- **Set Networking Goals**: Determine metrics such as the number of connections made, or the number of follow-up meetings scheduled.

- **Schedule Regular Networking**: Dedicate certain hours each week exclusively for networking activities.

- **Review and Reflect**: Regularly assess your networking tactics. Which are yielding results? Where is there room for improvement?

- **Adjust Strategy**: Based on your assessments, fine-tune your approach. Try new techniques or events if needed.

- **Remember the Long Game**: Recognize that networking is a long-term investment and the payoff may not be immediate.

Remember, effective networking for entrepreneurs and startups is not transactional, it's about building a supportive community around your business. It's your role to be proactive, persistent, and patient.

SCALING YOUR NETWORK AS YOUR CAREER ADVANCES

The Key Ideas

Leverage Existing Relationships

- Cultivate existing connections as they form the backbone of your expanding network.

- Reconnect with past colleagues and mentors; their evolution can benefit your journey.

Engage in Targeted Networking

- Identify key individuals in your field with the potential to enhance your career trajectory.

- Utilize industry events, conferences, and online platforms to meet these individuals.

Offer Value

- Approach new connections with a mindset of mutual benefit.

- Share knowledge, provide introductions, or assist with problem-solving.

Diversify Your Network

- Intentionally broaden your circle to include people from various sectors, industries, and backgrounds.

- Garner diverse insights and learn from different perspectives.

Embrace Digital Networking

- Leverage LinkedIn and other professional networking sites to maintain and grow your network.

- Engage with content, join groups, and participate in discussions.

Practical Implementation

- **Conduct a Network Audit**: Periodically review your contacts to assess the strength of relationships and identify gaps in your network.

- **Set Networking Goals**: Establish clear, achievable objectives for expanding your network, such as attending a specific number of events or adding a certain number of new connections each month.

- **Create a Networking Schedule**: Block off time in your calendar for networking activities to ensure you maintain focus on this aspect of your career development.

- **Follow Up**: After meeting new contacts, follow up promptly with a personalized note or email. Reinforce the connection and set the stage for future interactions.

- **Utilize Technology**: Employ CRM tools or networking apps to manage and remind you of important dates, follow-ups, and the interests of your contacts.

- **Stay Current**: Regularly update your knowledge and news of your field to remain an invaluable resource and contact.

Consistency and Evaluation

- **Regular Reflection**: Evaluate the state of your network every quarter. Consider the quality of new connections and the depth of existing ones.

- **Quality Over Quantity**: Focus on maintaining meaningful interactions rather than merely increasing the number of contacts.

- **Feedback Loop**: Seek feedback from peers and mentors about your networking style and approach. Adjust based on constructive criticism.

- **Adapt Strategically**: As your career advances, adapt your networking approach to stay aligned with your evolving professional goals.

- **Measure Success**: Define metrics for success such as the number of opportunities generated or the strength of key relationships, and assess progress regularly.

HANDLING REJECTION AND BOUNCING BACK IN NETWORKING

The Key Ideas

Rejection is an inevitable part of professional networking. It's not a reflection of your self-worth, but rather an occurrence to navigate and learn from. Handling rejection with grace ensures continuous growth and opportunities within your career.

- **Embrace the Reality:** Understand that rejection is a common experience in networking. It doesn't indicate failure, but opportunity for reflection and improvement.

- **Reframe Your Perspective:** View rejection as feedback, not a setback. It provides valuable insights that can shape your approach and strategies.

- **Resilience is Key:** Building resilience helps you withstand and recover from the difficulties rejection can present. It's the foundation for bouncing back stronger.

Practical Implementation

Actionable Steps for Overcoming Rejection:

1. **Acknowledge Your Feelings:** It's okay to feel disappointed. Give yourself a moment to process before moving forward.

2. **Seek Constructive Feedback**:

   ○ Request feedback from the person or entity that rejected you.

   ○ Analyze the information objectively to understand how you can improve.

3. **Develop a Learning Mindset**:

   ○ Each no brings you closer to a yes.

   ○ Identify lessons learned and incorporate them into your networking tactics.

4. **Cultivate a Support System**:

   ○ Build a circle of mentors and peers for emotional support and guidance.

   ○ Discuss your experiences and gain different perspectives.

5. **Refine Your Approach**:

   ○ Re-evaluate your networking strategy and make necessary adjustments.

   ○ Tailor your communication to better match your audience's needs and interests.

6. **Continue to Reach Out**:

   ○ Persistence is crucial; continue to engage with new and existing contacts.

   ○ Expand your network to increase the chances of finding the right fit for your goals.

7. **Celebrate Small Wins**:

   ○ Recognize and appreciate the progress you've made, even if it's incremental.

○ Celebrate the connections you've successfully made and the insights gained.

Quick Recovery Techniques:

• **Mindfulness Practice**: Use techniques like meditation or deep breathing to regain composure after facing rejection.

• **Positive Affirmations**: Remind yourself of your skills and successes to boost confidence.

• **Short Breaks**: Allow time for self-care to rejuvenate your enthusiasm for networking.

Consistency and Evaluation

Maintaining consistent efforts and regularly evaluating your networking strategy are vital to overcoming rejection and achieving long-term success.

• **Set Regular Goals**: Establish short-term and long-term networking objectives to maintain focus and motivation.

• **Track Progress**: Document your interactions, follow-ups, and outcomes to measure growth.

• **Adjust as Needed**: Be flexible and willing to alter your networking methods based on performance and feedback.

Periodic Review:

• **Assess Your Approach Every Few Months**: Reflect on what's working and what's not.

• **Solicit Feedback from Trusted Contacts**: Gain external insights into your networking style.

• **Re-evaluate Your Goals**: Ensure your networking objectives align with your career aspirations and personal development.

Remember, rebounding from rejection in networking isn't about eliminating no's, but about strengthening your yes's. Each interaction is a step forward, irrespective of the immediate outcome. Stay proactive, adaptable, and resilient—your networking journey is a marathon, not a sprint.

NETWORKING ACROSS DIFFERENT AGES AND GENERATIONS

The Key Ideas

Networking is a timeless skill that bridges gaps between ages and generations. To be proficient, you must appreciate the diversity and unique perspectives that each age group offers. Here's how:

- **Understand Generational Identities**: Recognize the values and communication styles of Baby Boomers, Gen X, Millennials, and Gen Z. Each has distinct preferences.

- **Leverage Technology**: Integrate technology tools preferred by younger generations with traditional methods favored by older groups.

- **Focus on Common Goals**: Despite age differences, professionals generally share common objectives. Identify and align these goals to foster collaboration.

- **Adapt Communication Styles**: Shift your approach according to the generational proclivities; some may prefer face-to-face interactions, while others lean towards digital communication.

- **Build a Diverse Network**: A varied network allows for a more comprehensive understanding of the professional landscape.

Practical Implementation

- **Research**: Study up on the social and professional tendencies of different generations.

  - Baby Boomers: Value personal interaction and strong professional ethics.

  - Gen X: Independent, resourceful, and value efficiency.

  - Millennials: Collaborative, tech-savvy, and favor work-life balance.

  - Gen Z: Socially conscious, mobile-native, and prefer fast, visual communication.

- **Communicate Effectively**: Craft messages that resonate. Be concise with Gen Z, engage Millennials with storytelling, maintain formality with Gen X, and prioritize relational depth with Boomers.

- **Mentorship Programs**: Implement cross-generational mentorship. Pair experienced professionals with younger ones, fostering knowledge exchange.

- **Networking Events**: Organize age-diverse networking opportunities. Mix traditional conference formats with interactive workshops.

- **Online Platforms**: Use LinkedIn for cross-generational presence and engage with different groups appropriately.

Consistency and Evaluation

- **Track Progress**: Regularly evaluate your network's generational diversity. Are you connecting across the age spectrum?

• **Quality Over Quantity**: It's not about how many connections you have, but the strength and diversity of these connections.

• **Seek Feedback**: Actively ask for insights from your network. Are your methods effective across ages?

• **Adapt and Evolve**: Networking strategies should evolve as demographics and professional environments change. Stay informed and flexible.

Networking across different generations requires adaptability, respect for diversity, and an ongoing commitment to personal growth and learning.

BALANCING ONLINE AND IN-PERSON NETWORKING

The Key Ideas

In an age where professional connections can be made with a click or a handshake, striking the right balance between online and in-person networking is crucial. You must leverage the strengths of both to forge meaningful relationships and advance your career. Here are the key ideas to keep in mind:

- **Integration, not Isolation**: See online and in-person networking as complementary, not separate strategies.

- **Strategic Presence**: Be selective about where you spend your time—online forums should align with your industry, and in-person events should be ones where you'll meet contacts of value.

- **Authentic Engagement**: Whether online or face-to-face, genuine conversations build stronger connections than transactional interactions.

- **Diverse Networks**: Aim for a rich tapestry of contacts from various industries and backgrounds; this diversity can lead to more innovative opportunities.

Practical Implementation

To practically implement a balanced networking approach, consider the following steps:

1. **Identify Goals** Set clear objectives for your networking efforts. What do you hope to achieve? Tailor your in-person and online activities accordingly.

2. **Optimize Online Profiles** Ensure your LinkedIn and other relevant social media profiles are professional, up-to-date, and reflect your networking goals.

3. **Curate Digital Connections** Engage with professionals in your field by following, commenting, and sharing relevant content. Initiate conversations that can lead to video calls or face-to-face meetings.

4. **Attend Targeted Events** Choose events, conferences, or meetups where you can meet influencers, future mentors, or peers in your industry. Prepare an elevator pitch and bring business cards.

5. **Blend the Approaches** After connecting with someone online, aim to meet in person if possible. Conversely, after meeting someone at an event, connect with them online to keep in touch.

6. **Quality over Quantity** Focus on forming a few high-quality connections rather than amassing a large number of superficial contacts.

7. **Offer Value** Always think about how you can help others in your network. This could be through sharing information, offering assistance, or making introductions.

8. **Follow Up** After any interaction, online or in-person, follow up with a personalized message referencing your conversation and suggesting a next step.

Consistency and Evaluation

Success in networking doesn't come overnight; it requires consistent effort and regular assessment. Here's how to ensure you stay on track:

- **Schedule Regular Activities** Dedicate time each week to online networking activities and attending events. Consistency builds visibility and recall among your network.

- **Set Measurable Milestones** Break down your goals into actionable milestones, like attending a certain number of events per month or making a number of new connections.

- **Review Interactions** Periodically, look back at interactions to see which have been fruitful. Refine your strategies based on what's working, and don't be afraid to drop what isn't.

- **Seek Feedback** Reach out to trusted contacts for feedback on your networking approach. They may offer valuable insights on how you can improve.

In closing, blending online and in-person networking can exponentially increase your professional opportunities. Implement these practices with authenticity and consistency, and you'll build a robust network that supports and enhances your career trajectory.

THE SYNERGY OF NETWORKING AND COMMUNITY SERVICE

The Key Ideas

Community service is not often the first thing that comes to mind when thinking about networking, but it's a powerful strategy. It builds genuine relationships and showcases your values.

Human Connection: At the heart of successful networking is human connection. Community service allows you to connect with like-minded individuals on a project with purpose.

Reputation Building: Aligning yourself with charitable work improves public perception. Others will see you as a contributor to the greater good.

Skill Development: Volunteering provides opportunities to develop new skills or enhance existing ones, which can be leveraged professionally.

Access to Opportunities: Involved in service projects can position you closer to unforeseen prospects, as you work alongside other professionals who could provide leads or references.

Authenticity in Action: Most people can spot insincerity. Volunteering is a way to put your values into action, which resonates with potential connections.

Practical Implementation

To integrate community service into your networking efforts:

1. **Select a Cause**: Choose a cause you're passionate about. Authentic interest fosters deeper engagement.

2. **Research Organizations**: Find local or online communities that work with your chosen cause and see what opportunities are available.

3. **Commit Your Time**: Schedule blocks of time for these activities. Regular involvement will help you form bonds.

4. **Engage Fully**: Be present and active. Don't just show up—participate meaningfully.

5. **Share Your Skills**: Offer your unique professional skills to maximize the impact of your volunteer work.

6. **Network Intentionally**: While the primary focus is service, remain open to making connections. Share your professional background when appropriate.

7. **Be Humble**: Project humbleness. Boasting about accomplishments can turn potential connections away.

Consistency and Evaluation

To make the most out of networking via community service, consistency is key.

Maintain Involvement: Regular participation increases your visibility and strengthens relationships.

Evaluate Connections: Periodically reflect on the connections you've made. Nurture the most promising relationships.

Measure Impact: Look at both the community impact and personal/professional development. The balance signifies a successful synergy.

Adapt and Grow: As you develop, your community service role may evolve. Stay flexible to adjust to more impactful positions or responsibilities.

In conclusion, merge networking and community service to craft a more meaningful professional journey. It's not just about whom you know but also about the difference you make together.

EXCLUSIVE NETWORKS: WHEN AND HOW TO JOIN

The Key Ideas

Exclusive networks are the echelons of the professional world. They provide unique opportunities for growth, learning, and connections. To access these circles, understanding the when and how is critical.

When to Join

- **Career Transitions**: Ideal if you're shifting industries or roles.

- **Scaling Your Business**: Seek exclusive networks when expanding your company's reach.

- **Seeking Mentorship**: Look to join when in need of guidance from industry leaders.

How to Join

- **Research**: Identify networks that align with your goals.

- **Value Proposition**: Be clear on what you can offer to the network.

- **Engagement**: Interact with the network's activities even before joining.

Practical Implementation

Step 1: Identify the Right Network

- Research networks that are relevant to your niche.

- Assess the exclusivity based on member success, industry impact, and barriers to entry.

Step 2: Prepare Your Application

- Highlight your unique skills, experiences, and what you can contribute.

- Obtain recommendations from existing members if possible.

Step 3: Engage with the Community

- Attend events or webinars hosted by the network.

- Contribute to discussions and showcase your expertise.

Step 4: Apply with Confidence

- Complete your application with precision, showcasing your understanding of the network's values.

Step 5: Wait for the Decision

- Exercise patience. Decisions in exclusive networks often involve deliberation.

- **Personalization is Key**: Tailor your communication. Remember details about people and reflect that in your conversations.

By adhering to these principles, you'll curate a network that not only supports your current standing but also paves the path for future opportunities.

Practical Implementation

Transform the above key ideas into tangible actions:

1. **Audit Your Network Regularly**:

   - Evaluate existing connections.

   - Shed those that no longer align with your career path.

2. **Engage Meaningfully**:

   - Comment thoughtfully on posts or articles shared by connections.

   - Initiate discussions on topics of mutual interest.

3. **Network Intentionally**:

   - Attend events selectively, with clear objectives.

   - Connect with purpose, aiming at a few significant interactions rather than many fleeting ones.

4. **Cultivate Relationships**:

   - Schedule regular check-ins with key contacts.

   - Celebrate their achievements and offer support through challenges.

5. **Be a Connector**:

   ○ Introduce people in your network who could benefit from knowing each other.

   ○ By doing so, you become a hub of your network, not just a spoke.

6. **Leverage Social Media Wisely**:

   ○ Use platforms to showcase expertise and share insights, selectively.

   ○ Engage with content genuinely, rather than just for visibility.

7. **Monitor your Time**:

   ○ Set aside specific times for networking activities.

   ○ Avoid networking becoming a disruptive presence in your day.

The key to practical implementation is to integrate these steps into your routine, transforming networking from a task into a natural part of your professional life.

Consistency and Evaluation

To ensure that your networking strategy remains effective, it's vital to maintain consistency and periodically evaluate your tactics:

- **Schedule Regular Reviews**: Once a quarter, assess the state of your network. Ask yourself what's working, what's not, and why.

- **Set Realistic Goals**: Have clear, measurable objectives for your networking activities, such as deepening three key relationships each quarter or attending one high-value event per month.

- **Adapt and Evolve**: As your career evolves, so should your network. Be open to new directions and opportunities to expand your professional circle in meaningful ways.

- **Feedback Loop**: Seek feedback from trusted connections about your networking style and approach. Use this to refine your methods.

- **Track Your Time**: Keep tabs on how much time you invest in networking. If it's disproportionate to the outcomes, recalibrate.

Remember, networking is not a destination but a journey. Regularly evaluating your approach will help ensure that the journey is purposeful, enjoyable, and beneficial to your professional growth.

ETHICS AND AUTHENTICITY IN PROFESSIONAL NETWORKING

The Key Ideas

Networking is a tool for professional growth, yet its effectiveness hinges on ethical behavior and authenticity.

• **Authentic Relationships**: Value genuine connections over transactional interactions. Prioritize quality over quantity in your network.

• **Transparency**: Be transparent in your intentions when interacting with others. Clear communication builds trust and long-term connections.

• **Mutuality**: Beneficial relationships are reciprocal. Provide value without the immediate expectation of a return.

• **Personal Integrity**: Uphold your principles consistently in networking situations. Compromising ethics for short-term gains undermines professional credibility.

• **Respect for Boundaries**: Recognize and respect personal and professional boundaries. Invasiveness can lead to strained relationships.

- **Privacy Consideration**: Treat other's information with confidentiality. Share judiciously and protect your contacts' privacy.

Practical Implementation

Putting these ideas into action involves mindful behaviors.

1. **Profile Honesty**: Ensure your professional profiles reflect your true skills, experiences, and intentions.

2. **Conversation Authenticity**: Engage in discussions with sincerity. Listen actively and respond thoughtfully.

3. **Value-Driven Interactions**: Before each interaction, consider how you can add value based on the individual's interests and needs.

4. **Feedback with Empathy**: Provide constructive feedback that respects the individual's feelings and professional stature.

5. **Recognition of Achievements**: Acknowledge and celebrate the accomplishments of your connections genuinely.

6. **Networking Plan**: Develop a networking strategy aligned with your ethical values, ensuring all actions are intentional and objective-driven.

Consistency and Evaluation

Continuous self-evaluation and consistent behavior reinforce ethical networking practices.

- **Reflect Regularly**: Take time to reflect on your networking interactions. Assess your authenticity and ethical behavior.

- **Solicit Feedback**: Ask for honest feedback from your peers about your networking style.

• **Set Benchmarks**: Establish personal benchmarks for ethical behavior and check your actions against them periodically.

• **Adapt and Evolve**: If inconsistencies are noted, take action to realign with your ethical standards.

• **Long-Term Mindset**: Understand that networking is a long-term endeavor. Authentic relationships cultivated ethically will yield the most sustainable rewards.

Remember, the value of your professional network is not just in the number of connections but in the depth and quality of those relationships which are nurtured through ethics and authenticity.

CRISIS NETWORKING: STAYING CONNECTED DURING TOUGH TIMES

The Key Ideas

Networking in the midst of crisis requires resilience, adaptability, and strategic thinking. When tough times hit, whether economic downturns, health crises, or personal issues, staying connected can become a lifeline. Here's what you need to know:

- **Prioritize Relationships:** Not all connections are equally pivotal in a crisis. Identify the relationships that can offer support, insight, or resources.

- **Leverage Digital Tools:** From social media to online conferencing platforms, utilize technology to maintain communication.

- **Offer Value:** Support your network by providing assistance, sharing opportunities, or simply listening.

- **Stay Visible:** Remain active in professional circles through virtual events, thought leadership, or engagement on professional platforms.

Practical Implementation

Implementing crisis networking strategies takes effort and consideration. Here is an actionable plan:

1. **Map Your Network:**

   ○ Categorize contacts by industry, expertise, and closeness.

   ○ Mark those who might be particularly relevant during the crisis.

2. **Regular Check-ins:**

   ○ Schedule periodic virtual meetups or phone calls.

   ○ Use these interactions to share updates and ask how you can help.

3. **Update Online Profiles:**

   ○ Ensure your LinkedIn and other professional profiles reflect your current situation.

   ○ Be transparent about looking for opportunities, if applicable.

4. **Contribute to Conversations:**

   ○ Join discussions in relevant professional groups or forums.

   ○ Share insights or offer solutions to problems related to the crisis.

5. **Learn and Adapt:**

   ○ Take online courses or attend webinars to upgrade skills.

   ○ Adapt your value proposition to the changing market needs.

Consistency and Evaluation

- **Set a Routine:** Dedicate regular time each week for networking activities.

- **Assess Interactions:** After each conversation or event, jot down key takeaways and potential follow-ups.

- **Adjust Tactics:** Based on feedback and outcomes, refine your approach.

- **Track Progress:** Use a simple spreadsheet or CRM tool to monitor interactions and outcomes.

In crisis moments, true networking strength shines through persistence and adaptability. Stay connected, remain empathetic, and foster your professional relationships even when times are tough. Your future self will thank you.

BEYOND THE BUSINESS: NETWORKING AND PERSONAL INTERESTS

The Key Ideas

Networking is a multifaceted approach to building professional relationships that extend beyond business transactions. Your personal interests and hobbies play a vital role in forging genuine connections and broadening your network.

- **Common Ground**: Finding shared interests with your connections strengthens relationships.

- **Authenticity Matters**: Be genuine when sharing and engaging with others about personal interests.

- **Long-Term Bonds**: Personal connections often result in longer-lasting business relationships.

- **Diverse Networks**: Involvement in varied activities expands your network beyond your industry.

Practical Implementation

Implement these strategies to integrate personal interests into your networking efforts effectively:

1. **Identify Common Interests**: Start conversations by discussing a range of topics, from current events to hobbies.

2. **Be Open and Curious**: Show genuine interest in the personal pursuits of others.

3. **Join Groups**: Participate in clubs or groups that align with your interests—these can lead to new and unexpected business opportunities.

4. **Host or Attend Events**: Organize or attend social gatherings centered around shared hobbies.

5. **Social Media Presence**: Use platforms like LinkedIn to share personal projects or achievements, fostering opportunities for connection.

6. **Volunteer**: Offer your time to causes or organizations that resonate with you, as they can be excellent places to meet like-minded professionals.

7. **Integrate Interests into Conversations**: Weave personal elements into business discussions to humanize and deepen engagements.

Consistency and Evaluation

Success in networking through personal interests requires a consistent and reflective approach. Regularly assess and adapt your strategies:

- **Accountability**: Set regular goals for making new connections based on shared interests.

• **Reflect**: Regularly reflect on how personal interests have influenced your network.

• **Feedback**: Seek feedback from your connections about the effectiveness of blending personal interests with professional networking.

• **Adapt**: In the ever-changing landscape of professional interactions, be willing to adjust your harmony of personal and professional lives.

By weaving your personal interests into your professional networking efforts, you ensure a more robust, diverse, and lasting network that can propel both your business and personal life forward.

MEASURING THE ROI OF YOUR NETWORKING EFFORTS

The Key Ideas

Measuring the return on investment (ROI) of networking is more nuanced than other business activities. It requires patience, strategic planning, and a long-term perspective. The following concepts are pivotal when seeking to gauge the effectiveness of your networking:

- **Defining Clear Objectives:** Understand what you aim to achieve from networking, be it building relationships, generating leads, or establishing thought leadership.

- **Quantifiable Metrics:** Track participation in events, number of meaningful conversations, follow-ups, and any referrals or business deals that result from them.

- **Time Tracking:** Record the time spent on networking versus the outcomes. Use this to adjust efforts for efficiency.

- **Quality over Quantity:** Focus on the depth and mutual benefit of relationships rather than sheer number of contacts.

- **Feedback Loop:** Gather feedback from peers and mentors to gauge your reputation in the network and the value you're providing to others.

Practical Implementation

To accurately assess the benefits of your networking activities, implement the following practices:

1. **Set Specific Goals:** Before attending an event or reaching out, define what success looks like. Examples include gaining three new business contacts or setting up two meetings for potential collaborations.

2. **Utilize CRM Tools:** Use Customer Relationship Management (CRM) software to keep detailed records of interactions, opportunities, and any resultant transactions.

3. **Use Surveys:** Post-networking event surveys can yield insights into the effectiveness of your communication and which areas may need improvement.

4. **Monitor Social Media Engagement:** Analyze likes, shares, and comments for content shared through professional networks like LinkedIn.

5. **Financial Analysis:** Whenever possible, tie networking efforts to revenue generated, considering the lifetime value of a new contact or client.

6. **Review and Reflect:** Regularly revisit objectives and adjust strategies according to what the collected data tells you.

Consistency and Evaluation

Ensuring that you consistently measure and evaluate your networking efforts is key. Remember:

- **Revisit Goals Regularly:** Adapt and refine your networking goals as needed.

- **Longitudinal Analysis:** Some relationships take time to bear fruit, so evaluate ROI over months, not just event-to-event.

- **Benchmarking:** Compare your networking ROI with industry standards or past performance for context.

- **Iterate Based on Data:** Make informed decisions to cease, continue, or alter networking tactics based on the data collected.

In conclusion, remember that networking is an investment. Like any investment, it requires careful tracking and analysis to understand its true value. Use these strategies to ensure that your networking is not just a social exercise, but a significant contributor to your professional growth and business success.

NETWORKING FAUX PAS: COMMON MISTAKES TO AVOID

The Key Ideas

Personalization Over Generic Interactions: Networking should be about meaningful connections, not collecting business cards. Take time to learn about individuals and personalize your interactions.

Listening vs. Speaking: Engage in active listening. It's not just about what you have to say; understanding others is crucial for building solid relationships.

Follow-Up Etiquacies: Prompt, thoughtful follow-up is key after meeting new contacts. Demonstrate that you value their time and the opportunity to connect.

Online Presence Management: Ensure your online profiles align with your professional image and are up-to-date. Inconsistencies can lead to distrust.

Respecting Boundaries: Understand and respect professional and personal boundaries. Avoid overstepping or making others uncomfortable with aggressive networking tactics.

Practical Implementation

1. **Craft Personalized Messages:** Tailor communications to show genuine interest. Avoid generic template messages, especially when reaching out on platforms like LinkedIn.

2. **Be Present:** At networking events, focus on the current conversation instead of looking over shoulders for the next opportunity.

3. **Provide Value:** Offer insights, help, or connections. Networking is reciprocal, not a one-way street.

4. **Use Social Media Wisely:** Share content that reflects your professional interests and expertise. Comment thoughtfully on others' posts.

5. **Prepare an Elevator Pitch:** Have a succinct and engaging summary of who you are and what you do, ready for new introductions.

Consistency and Evaluation

- Regularly assess your networking strategy. Are you maintaining relationships, offering value, and growing your network effectively?

- Keep track of connections made and the quality of interactions. Set periodic goals to develop these connections meaningfully.

- Reflect on feedback. Are people receptive to your approach? Adjust accordingly.

- Revisit your online presence every quarter to ensure it's reflective of your current professional goals and achievements.

Networking is an art that requires continuous improvement and attention to detail. By avoiding common mistakes and approaching each interaction with strategy and care, you can build a powerful professional network.

THE FUTURE OF NETWORKING: EVOLVING STRATEGIES FOR SUCCESS

The Key Ideas

Technology and globalization are redefining the scope of networking. The landscape is shifting from traditional face-to-face gatherings to a more nuanced hybrid of in-person, digital, and virtual spaces. As such, adaptability and technological proficiency have become essential.

- **Embrace Digital Platforms:** Cultivate an active presence on key professional networks like LinkedIn, and engage with industry-relevant communities.

- **Virtual Networking:** Leverage webinars, online workshops, and digital conferences as opportunities to connect with peers globally.

- **Personal Branding:** Use social media and content creation to establish thought leadership and a unique professional identity.

The foundation of successful networking remains rooted in authentic relationships. Strategic networking isn't just about expanding your contacts list—it's about nurturing genuine connections that can lead to mutual growth and opportunities.

- **Quality Over Quantity:** Focus on fostering deep, meaningful relationships rather than collecting contacts.

- **Diversify Your Network:** Connect with professionals from various backgrounds and industries to broaden your perspective and opportunities.

- **Follow-Up:** Keep in touch with your connections consistently, offering value and support, fostering lasting bonds.

Practical Implementation

To navigate the evolving networking landscape, start by integrating these strategies into your routine:

1. **Optimize Your Online Profiles:** Ensure your digital persona coherently showcases your skills, experience, and professional interests.

2. **Set Networking Goals:** Identify key figures in your industry you'd like to connect with and establish a plan for engagement.

3. **Use Technology to Your Advantage:** Familiarize yourself with networking tools and apps that can facilitate introductions and engagements.

Participate in online forums or contribute articles to industry publications to increase visibility and credibility within your professional circle.

- **Engage Daily:** Dedicate a portion of your day to networking activities, such as commenting on posts or joining discussions.

- **Host Virtual Events:** Gain visibility by organizing webinars or virtual meetups around topics of expertise.

Consistency and Evaluation

Consistently incorporating these tactics into your professional life is crucial for long-term networking success. Here's how you can maintain and assess your networking efforts:

- **Set Regular Check-Ins:** Schedule monthly or quarterly reviews to analyze the growth and engagement within your network.

- **Seek Feedback:** Ask trusted colleagues or mentors for input on your networking approach and areas for improvement.

- **Adjust Your Strategy:** Based on your evaluations, refine your approach to stay aligned with industry trends and personal goals.

Regularly refresh your knowledge and skills with the latest networking trends and technologies ensuring your strategies remain effective and relevant.

Remember: Networking is a marathon, not a sprint. It requires ongoing effort to maintain connections and adapt to new platforms and practices. With a clear plan and consistent action, you can cultivate a thriving professional network that propels your career forward into the future.

CONCLUSION

As we reach the end of "Mastering Professional Networking: 42 Best Strategies," it's essential to reflect on the journey we've taken together. From cultivating a networking mindset to navigating the future trends of networking, each chapter has been a stepping stone towards becoming a more proficient, proficiently adaptable, and resourceful professional.

Key Takeaways and Actionable Insights

Let's distill the essence of what we've learned:

- **Networking is a mindset**: Approach every interaction with openness, seeing potential in all conversations.

- **Goals are crucial**: Define what you want to achieve with networking to make your efforts more focused and productive.

- **Personal branding matters**: Cultivate a strong, memorable personal brand that encapsulates your values and expertise.

- **Listening is powerful**: It's not just about talking; active listening can lead to deeper connections and unexpected opportunities.

- **Online and offline balance**: Leverage social media platforms while cherishing face-to-face interactions for a holistic networking approach.

- **Mentorship is transformative**: Seek mentors and mentees to grow professionally and foster meaningful relationships.

Remember, networking isn't a one-off event; it's a continuous process of building and maintaining relationships that can lead to personal growth and collaborative successes.

Embrace the Future of Networking

Networking strategies evolve, just as industries and careers do. Stay adaptable, keep learning, and embrace new tools and platforms that emerge. The future may hold AI-driven networking opportunities or virtual reality-based conferences, further expanding our horizons.

Common Mistakes and Missteps to Avoid

- Don't overlook the importance of **ethics and authenticity**; genuine connections trump superficial exchanges.

- **Quality over quantity** counts: a few solid connections are more valuable than numerous shallow ones.

- **Rejection is not failure**; it's an opportunity to learn and refine your approach.

Networking as an Ongoing Art

Consider your networking journey not as a sprint to an end goal but as a marathon with evolving landscapes. Continue to enrich your professional tribe, listen actively, provide value, and adapt to the multicultural fabric of the global business community.

Measuring Outcomes

While networking might not always offer immediate tangible returns, remember to assess the qualitative aspects: increased awareness, stronger relationships, and professional growth. These indicators are often precursors to the more quantifiable benefits, like job offers, partnerships, and business growth.

Finally, as a seasoned professional with over two decades in the field, I offer you one last piece of advice: be patient and persistent. Networking is as much an art as it is a science. The fruits of your labor may not always be immediate, but with consistency and a sincere interest in others, you will see your world expand in ways you never imagined.

As we conclude, keep these strategies close at hand. Forge ahead with confidence, knowing that each connection you make, each hand you shake, and each conversation you engage in is a stitch in the intricate tapestry of your professional life. Networking is not just about climbing the ladder; it's about building a lattice of connections that supports and elevates everyone involved.

Remember, the end of this book is not the end of your networking journey—it's merely another beginning. Happy networking, and may your professional endeavors be ever fruitful and fulfilling.